Frightening New Furniture

KEVIN HIGGINS

salmonpoetry

Published in 2010 by
Salmon Poetry
Cliffs of Moher, County Clare, Ireland
Website: www.salmonpoetry.com
Email: info@salmonpoetry.com

ISBN 978-1-907056-25-3

Cover artwork: *Plastic Chairs* © *Steve Lovegrove* | *Dreamstime.com*
Cover design & typesetting: *Siobhán Hutson*
Printed in England by imprint*digital*.net

Published with financial assistance from the Arts Council

"Either the artist will make his peace with the darkness or he will perceive the dawn."

LEON TROTSKY
The Atlantic Monthly, October 1935

Acknowledgements

Acknowledgements are due to the following magazines, newspapers and anthologies in which some of these poems first appeared:

Magma, The SHOp, The Wolf, Natural Bridge (Missouri), *Coal City Review* (Kansas), *The Cork Literary Review, The Raintown Review* (New Mexico), *Salamander magazine* (Boston), *www.dissentmagazine.com, Nthposition.com, Democratiya.com, 3AMmagazine.com, ROPES, The Galway Advertiser, The Galway Independent, The Bish Yearbook 2008, Revival, Crannóg, Boyne Berries, Words On The Web, The Private Review* (online), *The Watchful Heart — A New Generation of Irish Poets — Poems and Essays* (Ed. Joan McBreen, Salmon Poetry, 2009), *Best of Irish Poetry 2009* (Ed. Paul Perry, Southword Editions).

Midnight Mass featured in Joe Geoghegan's *The Eye of The Beholder* exhibition at the 2008 Cúirt Festival of International Literature.

Contents

ONE—That Was My Country

TWO—The Lost Years

THREE—Clear Out

FOUR—Untidiness

FIVE—Getting Somewhere

Thursday, April 6th, 1967

The clock nudges three. Soon
the sun will move across the day's news.
For now, it lies in wait for me, unopened bundles
outside the corner shops of North London:

Decline in Soviet research efficiency.

Yesterday, New Orleans businessman,
Clay Shaw, pleaded 'Not guilty'
to conspiracy to murder
John F. Kennedy.

Che Guevara
has visited Bolivia twice recently
and is expected back soon.

Chelsea seek revenge on Sheffield Wednesday.

West Berlin police detain eleven students
for plotting to kill US Vice-President,
Hubert Humphrey.

In *The Guardian* crossword, Down 21
is four letters for a seaweed
found in East Anglia.

Today's weather: sunny intervals,
scattered showers, wind moderate or fresh,
locally strong. 10 degrees centigrade.

I kick my legs oblivious
to the politics and weather outside
this big, white place
I've landed in.

Tonight, I'll miss Engelbert Humperdinck
sing "Please, release me" on *Top of The Pops*,
and the ministerial broadcast by Mr Richard Crossman,
Leader of the House of Commons.
But I don't care.

I'm too busy sniffing the air,
and don't like the look of things here.
The room fierce with light. A trolley
rattling down a corridor telling me things
I don't want to hear.

St. Stephen's Day, 1977

for my mother

Yesterday, in my new football boots I moved
like Kevin Keegan through the silver afternoon.
Today, *Mull of Kintyre* is number one
and the film director Howard Hawks is dead.
I take my football boots off,
am myself again.

You're still a skeleton with all day night sweats.
The doctor, who knows the why of everything
but this, has given you back for Christmas.
Most of the turkey goes leathery in the fridge.
Dad puts the telephone down, tells me
to extinguish the TV. The doctor
wants you back three days early.

Our Ford Cortina cradles you
through late afternoon streets,
all those lit windows and wreaths.
But we don't see them. And nothing is said
as we deposit you at Unit Seven,
Merlin Park Hospital. You at the door
giving a small pale wave. In the near distance
the disused boiler's giant chimney stack.
The rain saying terrible things
as we drive off, that Christmas
you didn't die.

ONE
That Was My Country

1994 Revisited in the Shantalla Movie House

"The first recorded use of the phrase Celtic Tiger
is in a 1994 Morgan Stanley report by Kevin Gardiner"
Wikipedia

I am Kurt Cobain and Doctor Strangelove;
haven't yet had to choose
between putting the gun in my mouth
and developing a twitch
in my mad right arm.
All that is years away.

Live and let live, as I never say.
I am learning to love
the pragmatist within,
but won't yet name him.

I watch Ingmar Bergman films
on Monday afternoons
in a world before passports
or utility bills.
According to reports
the house red in the wine bar
down the road
is improving all the time
and the women are possible.

I discover the beauty of *Supervalu*;
am a cooked chicken,
        a bottle of *Blue Nun*
and some of the worst poems ever written.
I forget about the government
and hope they'll return the compliment.
I am fifty five pounds and sixty pence
per week and for once
have turned up just
as the party's about to start.

Insurance Salesman Remembers Life on The Dole

When weekday afternoons were spent watching
The Spy Who Came In From The Cold
with other men's wives. Those
upstanding other men, whose hard slog,
not soft option made them

the backbone of this country
(they'd like to tell you) when
one man's penal taxation
was another's lifestyle to which
you became accustomed. Now

they have their way,
and you're sentenced
to gainful employment for life; you
have to find time to screw
their wives at weekends instead.

Success

No longer content to have your life be a song
that once drifted just outside the top twenty;
you count the years wasted trying to gatecrash
a party that never happened. Look beyond
the woman who yesterday promised
implausibly blue weather; the friend
who'll spend tomorrow waiting in
for a kidney infection
he ordered over the Internet; past all

those deleted from the system the night
you spring cleaned your life
to the sign up ahead that reads
Welcome to the Medium Sized Time!
But in your Earl Grey tea still sometimes see
a world where success was sex in East Galway
the Sunday the clocks went back,
on a day you had no-one else to be.

Quality of Life

after Charles Simic

Today Polish waiters bring us more soup
than we're able for.

But I was happier then.

When I asked for soup
I'd get a bowl with
nothing in it.

We'd sit there for years,
our heads full of smiley, Irish thoughts,
gazing into our bowls
with nothing in them.

Each night we'd sing our anthem
"For these bowls with nothing in them,
may we be truly grateful",
and mean every word.

Saying 'Thank you' was big.
We spent our whole lives doing it.

Not like now.

Woman Spots Ex-Husband Collecting Signatures on Shop Street

He, who on Saturday afternoons traditionally gathered
    the week's resentments together
to make a bigger and greater
    hatred, today stands banging
the sad tambourine of his tongue–
    "But what about me!"
on a street that'll choose
    Nancy Reagan every time
over any revolution led by him.

    At ten to four
he realises, though the sight of him
    with that clipboard
and tiny green biro isn't quite
    her fantasy
of him being taken away
    by the forces of law and respectability
for bothering passersby outside
    the sex shop for change,
it's getting there;

    and retreats
to a bar loud with things
    he doesn't believe in
(like bottle openers and sunlight) to foam
    around the moustache about
how inauthentic the rain is, now Ireland's become
    this minimalist spaceship
where people just sip their decaffeinated water
    and listen to David Gray.

Another Monday

The calendar red with appointments.
I'm two more meetings before not enough
lunch; six hundred e-mails gone before
not enough mugs of tea in Calcutta;
an application form that must go
swift post before not enough coffee
in downtown Bogotá. I'm this
strategic handshake; all the rooms
I've ever worked and less.
Every hour Satan sends,
I spend warding off the ghost
of Monday morning future;

when the TV
will run recipes, economic forecasts,
penises up flagpoles and I won't
know what to say. I'll be
a motivational speech
that's lost its buzzwords
in a land of milk and toilet paper.
The afternoons I'll spend
mending her bras, and racking
the hard-drive for concrete examples
of my not-too-badness.

I'll miss out on the alternative rock explosion
of two thousand and thirty four.
Too busy arguing with the dead,
who, in the end, will all
turn out to be me.

Yesterday's Pinstripe Suit

Who'd once happily have driven
an oil and gas pipeline through
his own granny's front room; or
plopped a twenty storey car park
on the last sliver of green this side
of the Mad Cow Roundabout. His smile
several times investigated by
the Serious Fraud Office,
but they could prove nothing.
His catchphrase: "Today,
I'm jealous of myself."

In the day room he hums to himself
the theme from *Eastenders*; and
when the others have been shuffled
off to bed watches late night repeats of classic films.
Last night, Jimmy Stewart looked out a window.
Tonight, Janet Leigh steps into a shower.

He becomes the old address books
he carries everywhere with him
*(The number you have dialled
has been disconnected)*, there
with his memories, and then
some antiseptic afternoon
not even them.

You wake up one day
and find your whole life mislaid.

That Was My Country

after Carol Ann Duffy

The phasing out of stone walls and saints.
The statues not daring to move.
When there was planning permission
for anything and morning
was breakfast baps and gravel
going back that road by the truckload.
When transparency meant
the skirts just kept getting shorter.
We so believed in sunshine,
on rainswept days we'd carry sunglasses
on top of our heads,
just in case. Wherever we wanted to go
Ryanair would get us almost
there and the world was
not our problem.

We still have butter
on our *Rich Tea* biscuits
for now, but no more
Coconut Creams;
and everywhere statues
of virgins and freedom fighters
think about stretching their legs.

Cheap Polyester Suit

"nothing can be fixed, it is always the end"
Ronan Bennett

As the pills and loans run out,
and the world opens its eyes
to all the migraines and final reminders
it has coming; I can live

with grannies nationwide
being denied the traditional
new set of teeth for Christmas
or, as the crisis deepens, men in funny hats
upstairs killing Anne Frank;

but will not tolerate the general return
of instant coffee. And any toilet paper
not dipped in Aloe Vera will be
immediately sent back.

I'm the Friday night catastrophist
who, come Monday morning, goes in fear
of the cheap polyester suit my father
became in that land of petrol shortages
and new *Blondie* singles, that was
nineteen seventy nine.

Ourselves Again

In the park our ice lollies
fall victim to the June bank holiday heat,
while in glass rooms numbers moving
through dark computers
declare the future
finished.

Tomorrow, we'll have our double glazing
taken out; the crack put back
in the ceiling and a draught
installed under every door.
I'll attach a For Sale sign
to the seat of my pants.

Gangs of the angry unemployed
will bear down on the G Hotel
chanting "Down with *Daiquiris*
and *Slippery Nipples*! Give us back
our glasses of *Harp*!"

In pubs nationwide, the carpets of yesteryear
will be reinstated, and there'll be meetings
of Sinn Fein The Workers Party
going on permanently upstairs.

On our knees, we'll ask
for the unforgiveness of sins
and life not lasting.
We'll be ourselves again
and then some.

The Financial Times

with thanks to James Martyn

The fall in oil prices is a cup of cold tea
warmed slightly in the microwave.
Each morning brings
uncomfortable accounting situations.
MISSING FINANCIER FOUND BY F.B.I.
Royal Bank of Scotland — Making It Happen.
There is a hole
and the Corporate Enforcer is looking into it.
Another page in the epic:
The Great Unpleasantness of 2009
And How We Didn't Survive It.
This year, for their birthday, everyone gets
the blame. We find our trousers
repossessed and down around
somebody else's ankles.

Calls For St. Patrick To Come Out
Of Retirement

They slid back amongst us,
assigned dream paper values
to our small few acres.
The runny nose of history now
safely beyond use,
the snakes were rewarded
with Champagne and dickey bows
everywhere they went:
a twenty year Festival
of Acquiescence.

We wake
to enough concrete and glass
for another Los Angeles;
the snakes still hissing:
"Could we not wangle it?"
But their wangling days are done.
And there's no longer any such thing
as an acceptable level of snakes.
Those who yesterday accompanied them
in their two-seater sports cars, today
don't remember their names,
as the clenched fists shout:
"The end of snakes!
The end of snakes and now!"

Without

"He had come a long way to this blue lawn",

F. Scott Fitzgerald, *The Great Gatsby*

The picture is brilliant and he's in it.
Townhouses and apartments with a marina.
He never lets anyone go without.

A hotel in the Black Sea resort of Varna.
A twenty thousand square foot spa.
The picture is brilliant and he's in it.

Dubai's largest tourist hostel.
One hundred and nineteen villas.
He never lets anyone go without.

He's pre-approved for everything.
Crowds helicopter in for his birthday.
The picture is brilliant and he's in it.

Headlines, when one morning before
breakfast he buys the island of Ireland.
He never lets anyone go without.

Combined anticipated sales: € 500 million.
Developer's body found in shed.
The picture gone dark and him still in it.
He never let anyone go without.

March 5th, 2009

29

The Brother

While he slapped up multi-storey promises
to himself across most of the Near East,
I was busy being
between job. Who knew?
Ozymandias had a useless brother.

Or I had him. During his best years
I was all the cash
he lent me. He was in a meeting right now.
But I had hours.

Until the day he couldn't pay
the light bill, drank
deep the fumes from the Ferrari
he couldn't sell. I survive;

am the three legged kitten
who comes limping
adorably to your doorstep.

And you will give me milk.

2009

Cometh the year of no anaesthetic.

Every High Street from Twickenham
to Burnham-on-Crouch
is having its *Woolworths* taken out.

The talk is of Somali pirates
and bacteria in the tea towels.

Each new set of government statistics
are the worst figures ever.

On your shopping list you scribble
'salami' and 'razors'.

To fish finger or not to fish finger,
that is the question.

Someone texts to ask you to stop
the Holocaust against the Palestinian people.

A friend drops in to confirm
the ten years he's been away
wasn't long enough.

The world is a Christmas gift
the shop won't take back.

The New New Ireland

The traffic jams of old are being rounded up
and taken in for questioning. One by one,
our favourite restaurants disappear.
We whisper our tiny goodbyes
to the stuffed grape leaves of yore.

Yesterday is the money
we couldn't be bothered
to pick up off the floor.
The Collector-General rummages
down the back of our sofas
in the hope of loose change.

The taxi-driver says: "Didn't we survive
the Famine." Our *Red Bull* days
have delivered us to the guy
with the rubber glove
now standing over us:

"I am Quantitative Easing
and the only thing
you haven't tried."

Ice

You don't believe in the devil,
but before you can whisper
"full prostrate exam", here he is.
Sky fat with coming ice.

The barbecue over, you wake up
with no-one to carry your coffin,
but don't believe in the devil.

You do not exist,
but sit here making for yourself a past.
Sky fat with coming ice.

You're against going outside and against
anyone even thinking about going outside,
but don't believe in the devil.
Sky fat with coming ice.

Worse

for Niall O'Brolcháin

Airplanes fall unexplained from the sky.
The cat vanishes for a lost weekend
without end. The room fills up
with all the wrong people
and everyone's joining
the Church of Worse.
Everyone's joining
with all the wrong people
the room fills up
without end
for a lost weekend
the cat vanishes
unexplained
from the sky
fall airplanes.

TWO
The Lost Years

Birth of a Revolutionary

The boy who liked nothing better
than a Winter night spent hating
The Bing Crosby Christmas Special
eventually goes to the school disco;
spots the girl in the pink legwarmers
at the far end of the hall;
about her person, a youth
with at least two pairs of hands.

Not yet midnight.
Home. The boy goes upstairs.
In the morning someone else
will come down
and will not want his *Frosties*:
      Rebel Without Deodorant.
A young man destined to do his bit
to help the world into difficulty.

We would like to caution readers
this revolution contains scenes of banality
and an asexual nature...

The Recruiting Sergeant

"The old men and women of twenty"
Lenin

I am fifteen years old.
You're the man at the door with the plan:
how to overthrow Dad.
You whisper me the code words
'epoch', 'slump', 'transformation'.
Your blank expression swats off with ease
incorrect ideas. You're wise

as a roomful of Ayatollahs
and go through the years sticking to that;
never once distracted
by the false prophets of
it could be worse: your daughter
could have started going out with me;
your bum been smathered in gravy
and fed to Alsatians.

I am fifteen years old
and putting on the jacket
we'll spend the next decade
trying to make the world wear.

House Guest

after Elizabeth Bishop

For eighteen months
he's been staying
until the end of next week –
harder to pin down on any calendar
than the precise date of his world
uprising of the workers,
which he writes down for you nightly
on that day's anti-poll tax leaflet.

All the first week of January, fried slices
of the Christmas pudding his mother sent him
in the post are breakfast, lunch and dinner.
Work or the laundrette would get in the way
of his plans for the planet.
Your one bedroom flat is starting to smell.

When not away on a demo chanting
"Victory to Iraq!" his afternoons are spent
doing despicable things to worse women
in your bed. The pile of twenty pence pieces
on your bedside locker diminishes daily.

Yesterday, he was rushed to hospital
to have the y-fronts he's worn
for the past sixth months
surgically removed.

Today, he's what
emerges from your living room
sofa bed to tell you
where you're going wrong.

World Without Worry, Amen

Some pebble-dashed afternoon a doctor frowns,
says the girl I'm living with
in her mother's council flat
is not pregnant, just allergic to herself.
Dinner is something from the local chippie
but it was closed. The truth obvious

as a big, orange cat in a stripped winter tree
but I'm not having it. In the off-licence
I tell the one about the bloke who missed out
on the summer of love
because he was still caught up
in the panic of 1893.

That rattling cough, I shake off
with some antibiotics her mother got
for a septic foot, months
before I met them. I do not die today.

Our future: a bottle of white cider.
The thoughts I don't have,
I should keep to myself. Instead,
I ask her to marry me. *Yes.*
Next Wednesday week we'll begin
never having heard of each other.
It will last forever.

Ode To The Russian Revolution

after Warren Beatty & John Reed

Not the continent of tractor factories
you became. Nor the photographs of those
later killed by questions they didn't ask.

But the banners made of bed linen
flooding Nevsky Prospect. A boy's laughter
at an old man's shout of "Down with everything!"
on a street packed with serious talk.
Another man vanishing into the morning
with some odd vases of valuable porcelain.
The high white letters of the crowd's
new sounding slogans, as they move
around the corner on their way
who knows where.

Our End of Summer Holiday, 1989

for Sophie

In open revolt against alarm clocks
and free market economics, I decide
there's more to life
than dipping into the petty cash;
take early retirement at twenty two;
become the greatest accounts clerk
that never was. You're

the pause for reflection
which could last my whole life. Reckless
as a Chinese student facing down a tank,
I gamble the month's rent on our ten days
together. We begin with separate rooms, end
with you gone away on your different train.

I open the filofax and scribble *cancelled*
across the months I'd planned
to spend in your pants; hum
to myself my requiem
for an affair that never was,
before giving way
to two skinheads singing:
"We are white! We are white!
We are white!" on the Piccadilly Line
northbound platform. This

is where I slip through
the non-existent ice.
I spend the night in the bathroom
of a house I used to live in.
Down and out in Haringey and Enfield.
I'll sleep on various friends' floors
as the Berlin Wall gets ready to fall.

The Lost Years

Before I found the lesser poetry
of tax bills and unblocking the drains;
each Christmas Eve I was a pair
of disintegrated grey trousers, held
together by a socially concerned
safety pin. I'd emerge from the plane,
like a great historical event in the making,
with the ticket my mother sent me.

The rest of the year I was rumours
of sleeping bags on acquaintances' floors;
bounced cheques and borrowed fivers.
When challenged I was a suppressed sneer
at their small ideas and art of the probable.
I was the future they'd all one day wake up to;
and revolution meant more
than cheering on the bad guys
in *Die Hard* One, Two and Three.

Now, over breakfast I scour the Daily News
for oversized ideas and improbable tomorrows:
Students Waving Placards,
Whiskers For Slobadon Milosevic,
Anorexics Against Everything;
in daily instalments bequeath them
my rage at finding myself
lost to the lesser poetry
of tax bills and unblocking the drains;
nothing here to comfort me
but the complexity of an Israeli bomb
tearing a child's face off.

Days

We'd let the Daddy-long-legs take
the tower block hallway,
as we took time out
from demos in support
of those more fortunate
than ourselves
for a feast of taramosalata
on vintage brown bread
washed down
with the best can of *Kestrels*
a fifty pence piece could buy.

Our kitchen sink may have been
a failed utopian experiment;
the revolutionary group we'd just joined
a corpse passing wind.
But all we needed was
a draft to sit in
to talk about Agent Orange;
and with your rolled cigarettes,
my missing teeth,

we were insurgents waiting
to be hanged at dawn;
as we watched
the flat be torn apart
by a Keith Moon cat.
All dressed down
and someone to be.

Whatever happened to alienation?
Those were the days.

The Great Purge

An argument in which there was no
such place as Switzerland;
time to do unto others
and have it done to you.
Some woke up with their
throats cut; others
never came back
out of the bathroom.

But mostly the punishments were road signs
that read: *Topeka 560 miles,*
or *Welcome to East Sussex,* as we scattered
to become after dinner speakers;
hairspray salesmen in southern Illinois; or
end our days with nothing to declare
but our neutrality.

Hard to believe we were all
once in the same room, saying things like
"socialist transformation of society";
and then downing pints for the cause
on perfect Thursday evenings,
when the world was new
and *would* belong to us.

THREE
Clear Out

Hero

The day you fall, bawling into the world
in a village northeast of Salisbury;
in faraway Florida, Sidney Poitier is busy

being one day old. In Moscow heavily scarved
women mark the anniversary:
Lenin — One Month Dead Today.

Your two older brothers soon join him.
And your father, Gabriel, scarpers.
You are ten years old. It is nineteen thirty four

and all down to you. Mission schools,
then university. You are a teacher.
Your only son dies of cerebral malaria.

For subversive speech,
you are under arrest. Ten years.
You study law. The Party

chooses you. Rocket launchers
and Chairman Mao. You look in the mirror
one morning and see: His Excellency Comrade President.

Your name on the lips of a continent.
In the final act you start gifting
farms the white man stole

to your friends. One for everyone
in the audience. As the supermarket shelves empty,
your life fills up with dead people.

The country may be living on Styrofoam and grass
but will sing your name
one last time. The air fat with laughter

as you step into the TV to say
"We don't cheat; but on the other side…
all sorts of irregularities."

A foreign journalist is arrested
on the tenth floor
of a hotel near the airport.

Silence,
but for the sound of an occasional dog barking
on Samora Machel Avenue.

Outside your office the sign:
Mugabe is right. It is two thousand and eight
and all down to you.

The Country I Dreamt Up While Protesting On Shop Street

Land without loneliness or weather.
Even the old men do not complain.
Yesterday my quick signature abolished poverty.
This morning my handshake ushered in
a new era of international happiness.
Women in provincial laundrettes wear
fantastic smiles. For their own good
schoolchildren are force fed my wife's
Complete History of Everything.
I can tolerate anything,
except being contradicted.
In the redesigned town square
rogue elements line up to confess.
It will be years yet before even a drunk dares
to stop and ask one of my statues a question.

Letter To A Full Time Revolutionary

Your latest outfit an arrangement in grey.
You'd vanish into the wallpaper,
but for the chopping movement
your hand makes as you strike
just the right note;
wax ideological, now
Venezuela, now
the latest interest rate rise;
put on a human voice to tell us
about the old woman left
to die in her own mess
on the twenty first floor
of a tower block named after
the bloke who started
the Boer War.

I was once you.
The agreed candidate,
who emerged inevitably
from a thinly carpeted room;
mouth crammed
with all the right slogans.
You get by on a diet of
abstract concepts:
       United Fronts
with some Workers' Democracy
on the side; nightly pray for
a stock market crash: dream
of billionaires going out
tenth floor windows.
Your exclusion proceedings
will be precisely minuted
by someone you recruit
tonight. I was once you.

Unmade

Paradise has taken a beating.
Dawn raids on houses I used to live in.
The ghosts of my unmade friends gather.
Out for the evening, I end up in a taxi
the man with curry on his jacket.
Or, alone with my armchair hatreds,
I sit here hoping Dick Cheney will phone.
Dick Cheney will phone I sit here hoping.
Or, alone with my armchair hatreds,
the man with curry on his jacket
I end up in a taxi. The ghosts
of my unmade friends gather.
Dawn raids on houses I used to live in.
Paradise has taken a beating.

Clear Out

Today it all goes to the dumpster,
my old political furniture:

the broken bookcase called
nationalisation of the banks;

the three legged dining chair called
critical support for the P.L.O;

the fringed, pink lampshade called
theory of the permanent revolution;

the collapsed sofa-bed called
excuses we made for Robert Mugabe;

the retired toilet seat called
the trade union movement.

And the man who spent
twenty five years sitting on it?

At three thirty six pm
in the stripped living room

I forget him. As of now
he never existed.

I'm too busy watching
the delivery man unload

frightening, new furniture
from that van pulled up outside.

June, 2007

Comrades

"As an ex-member of the Militant Tendency I wanted to bring down the State that most people supported. I'm glad the likes of me…were prevented from doing so…Thank you Special Branch."
Stephen Brent, Chichester on the BBC website

1981. Capitalism was a Dimplex heater
with a broken switch. We'd
rush across the greasiest Formica,
the nastiest carpet to agree with each other
and cheer the news: *redundancies rocket,
stock markets on the floor.*

"Another Tory government
is out of the question," you told me.
It was February, 1982. The daffodils
couldn't have cared less.

"This puts a question mark over
Thatcher," I told you.
It was November, 1989. Hailstones
on Stoke Newington High Street.

Today, we meet with a history
of fried bread and picket lines
behind us. We believed in each other.
Now, it's a hundred years

since those afternoons
full of sunlight and clenched fists
when—in miners' strikes and poll tax riots—
we were like boys playing
in hoped for snow.

Retired Revolutionaries Reunion; or Whatever Happened to the Far Left Threat

As the peanuts arrive
in a Charles and Camilla commemorative ashtray,
we who've long since retreated
behind well trimmed hedges to write
poems that double as instruction manuals
for clean liberal living; settled

for the consolation prize
of being found alive
under a pile of coats with *Miss Mullingar,*
First Runner Up, 1981; or swapped

our socialism for honest jobs
selling slaves over the internet, move with ease
among the watercress sandwiches. Until the guy
with the *Jobs Not Bombs* t-shirt stands
in the middle of the room,

like an answer to a question
no-one wanted to ask; raises his glass
as he talks (*no-one listening*
and no-one going to listen) about how, comrades,
life was once—for five whole minutes—
this dream Cup Final in which our side
was one, two, three, four...
so many goals ahead
          it was ballet dancing.

Revolt

His world cracked like a brandy glass,
when she said she was leaving, had
met a man not yet beyond repair.
The universe chuckled and moved on,
not wishing to afflict the mocked. Now,

he texts her to say he thinks he left
his life's work in the back of her car; and
though the rabble-rouser she married
vanished around 1975, he's still against
poverty on Wednesdays. She replies

she should have known: inside
yesterday's perfectly sculpted revolutionary
was always today's paunchy liberal who slugs
his cabernet, and watches daytime TV
with an elderly Labrador named
Adlai Stevenson, the Fourth.

Don't Cry For Me

I'm Maude Gonne
in an off-brown trousers suit.
Whatever the issue, I'm an orgy
of outrage on the morning radio.
At every gathering of the disenchanted,
I'm a one woman politburo.
My wit legendary: friends reminisce how
I once assisted in the telling of a joke.

I'm the one who makes you opt
for the guy in the greasy suit.
Tomorrow, you'll brush him off
like dandruff. Choose me
and I'll go on; at the age of
a hundred and three
be wheeled onto state TV.
All croaky voiced, tell you
that as of 3pm next Thursday
I'll be handing absolute power
to my sister. I'm the hope

that makes you wish it was 1936
and you'd just been dropped
from a Lubyanka Prison
tenth floor window.

Stage Left

He's a pair of steel-toe-capped boots
marching on the British Embassy.

He's a one day general strike
thirty years ago last Wednesday.

He's a leaflet shoved into your hand.
He's May Day 1975.

He's an abstract discussion
about who to support
in a hypothetical war
between fascist Brazil
and democratic England.

He's something that almost happened
once: a proof copy
of a might have been masterpiece,
full of misprints.

He's a glass of red wine before breakfast
the day he decided
to fall down the stairs.

Even My Dreams Are Mediocre

Perfection is an evening of setting off smoke alarms,
love, going upstairs to smear each other
in cat food and curry.
"Change your life": Rilke tells me;
incapable of this, I put on
a new pair of socks instead. My face
the poster for a failed revolution.
We end up being ruled by overly reasonable
Swedes who give me a start
your own funeral parlour grant.
One by one, the whole neighbourhood go off
in my award winning plywood coffins.
"At last", Mother whispers, "You're
someone", as I nail her into her box.

Man Disappointed By History

The rain you predicted refusing to fall.
The International Workers of The World
storming garden centres everywhere
and not burning them down!
There have been implications
and you don't like them.

The next stop after Angryville
is Angryville again. You could
take up vodka or chocolate; spend
winter evenings trying to light the fire
with the obituaries of friends.

But rather than walk off stage,
you leave us wanting
less. Everything is a national
disgrace. Your daydreams furious
with pictures of those who arrive in Athens
around midnight to live the life
you're not; you whistle to yourself
your anthem: Will Get Fooled Again.

Wife Writes a Letter

Right now our plans for the future
     are crows converging
on a mortuary roof.
     From the weather
to the inflation rate
     most things here
he doesn't like them.

     This morning he railed
against communism and having
     to mow the lawn;
I began the six day war
     of my menstrual cramps.
Tomorrow we have
     the cat put down.

He's applied for a job selling
     contaminated meat
to hospitals and schools
     in the American Midwest.
He says it's time he started
     not making a difference.

The Big Conversation

It has been too long.
Your wife has left you for God
and Alcoholics Anonymous. Mine
is seven hundred miles away
and enjoying the quiet.
We crowd the coffee table
with things we hate: Piers
Morgan and your distinctly
unMexican neighbour
who goes about the place
in a poncho.

You say, humanity
is a child in the back of the car
demanding answers
it's delighted not to get.
No. We are not there yet.
I say, the world needs doors
behind which things can happen.
*We demand secrecy. Down with Freedom
of Information!* Later, we solve
the Middle East; decide, on balance,
not to nuke Saudi Arabia. Around five a.m.
I wake up stranded in front of this
twenty eight inch flat screen TV.

Recoil

You arrive in the morning with a bottle
of scotch and request for a loan. I haven't
been outside for a year. The last time
I spoke to *myself* was February
and that was through
an intermediary.

We go down the motorway backwards,
revisit We Have All The Answers,
pass the place Stitch Up, Treachery
and Assassination refused to recognise
themselves in the mirror.

By the time we get back it's obvious:
if we were with the Devil all along,
the other guy must be God.

Manifesto

I won't settle for
better.

I want a President
who'll give us wars
I can be against; live
for the beauty of bombed Afghan
wedding parties justifying
everything I think.

The international banking system
now a pair of old boots
with the soles worn away;
you will listen
when I tell you:
everything is not for sale.
Even if you paid me, I'd go
nowhere.

Activist's Lament

Scotch tape and anthrax.
Yellow alerts and Michael Moore.
Hanging chads and Scooter Libby.
Non-sequiturs and orange jumpsuits.
"Let's just say where they are now
they won't be bothering us." Vice
President Cheney offering
himself the contract. "In Texas
we just call that walkin'."

Two thousand nine hundred
and twenty two days of saying no
to you has left me hopelessly
in love with what you provoke. Tonight
I smile along with the rest,
as history takes a red pen
to my dreams of more. Inside,
I'm six years old and watching
the bouncy castle be taken away
after the best birthday ever.

This morning, for the last time,
the whole table listened when I spoke.
Tomorrow, I begin my new career
as a set of wind up chattering teeth
abandoned years ago in the bottom drawer.

His Hour Come Round At Last

"What's the alternative?"
Condoleeza Rice

The Central Bank has declared a moratorium
on new sitting rooms and laughter, all relics
of the bygone bourgeois age known as
the week before last. The dog starts to hum
something by Woody Guthrie. These
are our *Grapes of Wrath* days. We'll
pack what we can into an old jalopie;
from now on live in a black and white
photograph by Dorothea Lange.
Tomorrow, we'll hang.

People will look at us in museums;
wonder what it was like
to be here, watching the guy
who's spent the past twenty years
turning himself on with pictures
of queues for government issue
Cup-a-Soup, blowing his nose
on other people's sleeves
reach for the alternative economic strategy
he keeps in an old Aldi bag;
when you'd rather anything
than live in a world where
he has a point.

Seriously

Tomorrow will collar your enemies
against the iron railings of History.
These are the weeks of cold tuna fish pie.

You are serious as Herman Hesse
and bedsits smelling of cabbage.
Tomorrow will collar your enemies.

You're serious as all three stanzas
of *Deutschland Uber Alles* sung backwards
against the iron railings of History.

Serious as all two hundred and sixty four
episodes of *Murder, She Wrote*.
Tomorrow will collar your enemies.

This morning the heretic sky
throws down gold you cannot use.
But tomorrow will collar your enemies
against the iron railings of History.

Pact

Bad things,
I'll be against them.
If you'll be my friend, I'll give you
my sympathy for the Palestinians.
If you take down your pants, you'll get
my *don't get me started*
on George W. Bush.

Into my mouth you can drop
any slogan you want—
weekly on the letters page
I'll give you hate mail
you can only agree with—
if you'll sign up
to know nothing about
the games I play with children
in the shed at the bottom of the garden.

Let me in,
Alliance Against Everything, and together
we'll make of the world a girl
come to terms with the iambic beat
of my tobacco flavoured fist.

Dichotomy

Answering the door, the face
    which says its owner
down the years
    has done great work
for unworthy causes;
    time and again sided
with Death against Life
    and lost.

In the garden, a young cat
    having its first summer. Now
picks a fight with its own tail
    in the unkempt grass.
Now climbs a tree
    to debate world affairs
with the crows.

FOUR
Untidiness

Bookshop Romance

The girl behind the counter whispers: "Yes, Mother",
then puts the phone down with a cosmic sigh.
You look up from your D.H. Lawrence.
Something rustles in your corduroy trousers.

You want to shout: "Let me through!
I'm an existentialist"; to take her hand
and tell her: your own family Christmases
often resemble the aftermath of an embalming;
that your brother's a fully paid-up member
of *V-neck Sweaters for the Bomb*;
that most years you honour them
with your absence.

That you'd like her to come up
this evening to see your haiku
and the life you keep
in the shoebox under the bed.

That you've been admired
by women with bad judgment
all your life...

The Woman Who Tried To Be Fascinating

You took your rubber duck and dipped it
in the Caspian Sea; crossed the Gibson Desert
in a van full of ponchos and beards;
played tiddlywinks in Timbuktu
with a retired traffic warden who thought
he was the ghost of Josef Stalin. Back home,

you decorate your life with authenticity;
fill your timber frame house
with patchwork quilts
and poets with nothing to offer
but catarrh and unpaid bills.
After dinner they all line up to pee
in the multi-coloured pot
you had sent from somewhere so exotic,
no-one's ever been there.

The curtains close on you
in your wicker chair, wondering
why no-one told you: fascinating
is the new boring. On your lap, a stray cat
dying to whisper in your ear: "wherever
you go, you bring yourself."

Himself

after Simon Armitage

His big bald head was a deposed Prime Minister
sent to live by the seaside.
His laughter was a patch of sunlight
where the cat remembered California.
His 'goodnight' was a guru watching his last disciple leave.
His brand new sweater was a clerical error
that happened just before lunch on a Wednesday.
His favourite poem was a personal ad:
"Ugandan Male, 36, seeks white woman, 18-21.
     Must Be A Non-Smoker".
His sexual preference was none of the above.
His political views were the bit
that just wouldn't flush down.
His line of argument was a room with nothing in it
except a fat man full of *Supermacs* food.
His mouth was a letterbox
with a gale force wind blowing through it.

His end was a hard-boiled egg,
that was still warm when they found him.

The Athenry Man

"I left him to himself, which really means to others."
My Life, Leon Trotsky

Before her, he was all potential
like a block of half built apartments in Bulgaria.
She was the woman who saw in his eyes the sign
Huge Discount; that the world was a joke

he didn't quite get. Now, when his mother
malfunctions or the shower gets cancer
she does all the talking; leaves him
to his twelve hour shifts testing

catheters. She's the cup of coffee
that'll carry him through pandemics
and traffics jams; will spend Saturday night
letting him put it anywhere he wants

and still have him up and poured
into a white cotton shirt in time
for ten o'clock mass. She's
where he's been headed

since the doctor glancing
at the midwife said: "It's a shadow.
We just don't yet know
whose."

Midnight Mass

For one night only, everyone who's anyone
joins everyone who's not. His Worship, The Mayor,
thoughtfully scratches his left nostril, as the choir grapples
with *Jesus, Joy of Man's Desiring* by Johann Sebastian Bach.

Until the altos give way to an outbreak of shuffling feet,
a distant fit of coughing; and the Bishop steps forward:
"Our thoughts now turn to those who, during the past year,
have gone to that better place." For a moment the whole town
shuts its eyes. Mine stay open and focus on some of those
who've gone nowhere.

For whom my prescription, this time last year,
was *take carcinogens several times daily*
and don't get back to me; who by now should at least be
shuffling into their seats, like autopsies waiting to happen; or
sheepishly offering me the sign of peace
with big gangrenous hands;

who've turned up tonight looking absolutely fine,
when all year I've imagined worms having, for starters,
their right eyeballs before moving on to the main course
of brain.

Snapshots From A Lost Age

The time you found a peanut
under the kitchen table, and thought
that's dinner for this week sorted; or
turned up at the office in a diving suit complete
with pink luminous flippers, muttering
"I'm not weird. I'm what's really going on
in most people's minds." Those golden
pint of whiskey afternoons, before
the Letters To The Editor began. Now

your people skills are the place
Basil Fawlty meets Idi Amin.
Your dinner parties Nuremburg rallies
no-one turns up at. You're
out there for good, shouting
at the weather to end.

Bank Holiday Monday

The corner shop radio mutters to itself:
motorbike accident, attempted suicide,
as a woman buys flowers for
herself, then vanishes into
the traffic and polyurethane.   .

And somewhere a man with
no mind left to make up sings
antique songs to himself on a day
of straight down rain and closed
Chinese takeaways; remembers

when life was the miracle
of April snow, and he was more
than a strange car hesitating
sometimes at the end of her road.

To A Discarded Lover

after Fleur Adcock

Since I last saw you,
I've lived a completely normal life.
Your voice was a small meow
at a sad window; our days rye cake;
our nights chicken korma
and up against the wall. Like the Korean War
your mood swung one way,
then the other. If we were a book
we'd be The Weimar Republic:
The Final Five Minutes. Last I heard
you were arrested for trying
to bribe a government official
with old Finnish currency.
You turning up anywhere is like
a canary dying in a coalmine.
Nothing to be said but prayers.
Nothing to do but exit.
Mine is a shortlist you'll never make.
But when some judge finally
sends you to the electric chair,
I'll buy your hair on eBay,
carry it everywhere with me.
Our days were rye cake;
our nights chicken korma
and up against the wall.
Your voice a small meow
at a sad window.
Since I last saw you, I've lived
a completely normal life.

There You Go

Like a fanatic who's finally grabbed hold
of the microphone,
                    there you go.
And all I can do is sit here and wonder
whatever became of the one
who'd always laugh at the silliest things:
        Kajagoogoo's Greatest Hits
or him next door
taking his penis extension for a walk. If only
you'd stop,
            I'd ask you where she's gone.
But you go on, like October saying a bitter goodbye
on a night when no-one else walks the Salthill prom.

Untidiness

Not enough that I now
Winter in the Seychelles;
    have changed my name to Beau
and developed an evil twin
    brother called Clint.

Even here, there are days slow
    as bureaucracy, when I ignore
the passing butterflies
    to dream up a movie in which

your years scrubbing floors
    at a ball bearing factory
on the outskirts of Tirana end
    with your skeleton
being donated to charity.

Because life is untidiness
and then only the end
    of untidiness.

Nemesis

A down to the last bit of toilet paper type of day,
I lose my hat, gloves and mobile phone;
should go back to change the cat litter
and unblock the kitchen sink,
but instead catch the last bus out

track you down
to somewhere between here
and the far side of Bratislava;
tap on your door
and when you answer say:
"Last night I prayed to a statue
of Zhang The Venomous, and this
is one of the wishes he granted me."

All the days you played with my discretion,
as a child would with an elastic band,
explode briefly between us.

FIVE
Getting Somewhere

Newbolt Road, London N5:
Two Self-contained Flats

Through the letter box a leaflet
asking The Occupier to please
give generously and often to
the Make Poverty Permanent campaign;
and a card from the redhead
late of upstairs,

who once opened her door
wearing only a smirk, and
invited you in to check
the alignment of her pelvis,
when all you wanted
was a teabag;

who weeks later tapped
on your bedroom window
with a tub of taramosalata – marked
best before three months ago –
offering to spread it all over you
and not lick it off:

Tonight the Indian Ocean is its usual green.
My new found friends are away
doing fascinating things
in very loud voices; I'm sending this
on the off chance

you're still downstairs
threatening to write that book:
'Overcome Self-doubt
By Realising How Dumb
Other People Are' .

The weather is here,
and I'm nice, love
her late of upstairs.

A School Boy Goes Home Early

Twenty five years after me, you moved
through a chaos of blue uniforms
down those same break time corridors
towards the day you became
a list of things that'll never now happen.
Parties you won't be going to.
Cities you'll never visit.
A wedding day at which
you'll never arrive.
You couldn't see
that even the worst weather
of your worst day
would have given way
to something else;
that you could have lived
through anything
but this.

Postcard from New York

The Chrysler building is a golden rocket
    ready for the off.
The Empire State spends the evening
    trying on its blue hat.
At Grand Central Station
    Chinese pensioners play sad songs
of the old country on strange
    string instruments. Then pancakes
with syrup and snow
    on Lexington Avenue
the morning after the New York Giants
    win the Super Bowl.

I think of you and the life you've made
    in the letters page of The Skibbereen Eagle;
how you move towards terrible news,
    like a hagfish to a dead whale. Your views:
the same piece of rusty galvanise
    tossed around stormy night after
stormy night. From here on in
    this silence

is the sound of me not caring. Your life
    may be a house full of wonky
coffee tables, two legged chairs...
    cheap when you bought them
and that was years ago. But when
    I pull back the curtains on
tomorrow, whatever
    it throws my way,

I will not be listening to the wind.

Getting Somewhere

Turning forty two is like passing
through Portarlington on the train.
I will get somewhere eventually.

Today's paper says the everything
that was mine to win is now
the something I have to lose.

My daydreams busy
with clocks and budgets; I'm a man
destined to turn up early

for my own funeral, to spend
the morning redoing my tie
and wondering where the hell
everyone else has got to?

Relaxation Techniques No. 1

We could have waited for the Cappuccino,
the Soya Mocha to come;
but after the week we've had (seven solid days
of typographical errors and inconsolable rain)
a quickie in the café, love in the loo
was just what the Maharishi ordered.
A million muscles relaxing at once.

China

At the door, two small people
watch summer end. That morning
for the first time the scratching
sound which would grow
to become the whole world.
Dinner last night was fine
apart from the fact I was there.

Somewhere else, the weather is exploding,
and it is going to explode.
Your body language says
you'd rather be grabbed
in the hallway by a man
wearing an astronaut's helmet,
than accept a back rub from me.

Today, I turn fifty;
you fly to China. At the exact
moment your plane hits
the runway in Shanghai,
a friend phones to say
he's not dead, just isn't
speaking to me, while
at the other end of the kitchen
the people in the radio debate
toxic sludge in local lakes.

Together In The Future Tense

On a day that, for now, sits
unopened under the tree,
you'll push me uphill in a wheelchair;
say things like: *Augustus John,*
as you'll know, was obsessed
with motorcars and think
people know what you mean.

Every other Wednesday
we'll take the wrong medication
(you, mine and I, yours)
and the results will be
magnificent. I'll be forever answering
the question before last.

In our thoughts we'll commit
grotesque typographical errors:
for *Athens* read *Athenry*, for *Ralgex*
read *Canesten*, for *Disabled Toilet*
read *World Weightlifting Championships,*
for *Swan Lake* read *Loughrea.*

The once absolute monarchy
of my brain will grant autonomy
to my bits. Our bladders will be busy
writing their declarations of independence.

We'll be our very own festival of befuddlement;
as the light on the Aegean Sea
becomes a small boy
taking his ball home for the evening,
and the stray dogs wander off.

About the Author

Kevin Higgins is co-organiser of Over The Edge literary events. He facilitates poetry workshops at Galway Arts Centre; teaches creative writing at Galway Technical Institute and on the Brothers of Charity Away With Words programme. He is also Writer-in-Residence at Merlin Park Hospital and the poetry critic of the Galway Advertiser. His first collection of poems *The Boy With No Face* was published by Salmon in February 2005 and was short-listed for the 2006 Strong Award. His second collection, *Time Gentlemen, Please*, was published in March 2008 by Salmon. One of the poems from *Time Gentlemen, Please*, 'My Militant Tendency', features in the *Forward Book of Poetry 2009*. One of the poems in this collection, 'Ourselves Again', appeared in *Best of Irish Poetry 2009* (Southword Editions). His work also features in the *The Watchful Heart – A New Generation of Irish Poets* (Ed Joan McBreen, Salmon Poetry) & in *Identity Parade – New British and Irish Poets* (Ed Roddy Lumsden, Bloodaxe, 2010).